OF THE
PRIME MINISTER

University of
Chester

This boo
belov
boc
—

Planning and Access for Disabled People

A good practice guide

**Prepared for the Office of the Deputy Prime Minister
by Drivers Jonas**

March 2003
Drivers Jonas
Office of the Deputy Prime Minister: London

Office of the Deputy Prime Minister
Eland House
Bressenden Place
London SW1E 5DU
Telephone 020 7944 4400
Web site www.odpm.gov.uk

Further copies of this publication are available from:

Office of the Deputy Prime Minister Publications
PO Box 236
Wetherby
LS23 7NB
Tel: 0870 1226 236
Fax: 0870 1226 237
Textphone: 0870 1207 405
Email: odpm@twoten.press
or online at www.planning.odpm.gov.uk/index.htm

ISBN 1 85112604 X

Contents

Foreword

The Government is fully committed to an inclusive society in which nobody is disadvantaged. An important part of delivering this commitment is breaking down unnecessary physical barriers and exclusions imposed on disabled people by poor design of buildings and places. Too often the needs of disabled people are considered late in the day and separately from the needs of others.

We want to change that. We want the needs of disabled people properly considered as an integral part of the development process. As our July 2002 document **Sustainable Communities: Delivering through planning** made clear, the land use planning system has a key role to play in creating and sustaining mixed and inclusive communities.

This good practice guide, stemming from a recommendation of the Disability Rights Task Force, describes how all those involved in the development process can play their part in delivering physical environments which can be used by everyone. It encourages local planning authorities and developers to consider access for disabled people, and stresses the importance of early consultation with disabled people, when formulating development plans and preparing planning applications.

The guide explains the relevant legislation and policy frameworks, shows how local planning authorities can put in place appropriate planning policies and development control processes, and suggests ways in which these can be implemented and enforced effectively. It pinpoints the role of developers and occupiers and underlines the benefits to them in providing environments which are accessible and inclusive. A clear message is that this makes good economic sense as well as being socially responsible.

I hope that this guide will raise awareness of the issues and encourage everyone involved to embrace the advice and good practice pointers to help create buildings and places which disabled people can use with dignity and confidence.

Tony McNulty
Parliamentary Under Secretary of State
Office of the Deputy Prime Minister

Part 1

A summary of
Good Practice Points

1. Introduction

1.1 This guide makes a number of key suggestions. A summary of the suggestions or **Good Practice Points** is given below. The reader should refer to the full text of the guide for a more detailed explanation.

1.2 A general point of good practice

> **Good Practice Point 1:** p18
>
> All parties involved in the planning and development process should recognise the benefits of, and endeavour to bring about inclusive design.

1.3 A summary of good practice for determining authorities

> **Good Practice Point 2:** p33
>
> If a development proposal does not provide for inclusive access, and there are inclusive access policies in the development plan and in supplementary planning guidance, bearing in mind other policy considerations, consider refusing planning permission on the grounds that the scheme does not comply with the development plan.

> **Good Practice Point 3:** p34
>
> Include appropriate inclusive access policies at all levels of the development plan supported by a specific strategic policy. Do not rely on a single access policy.

1.4 A summary of good practice for developers, occupiers and owners

Good Practice Point 18: p71

- Adopt a corporate policy that requires inclusive design to be part of all concept briefs to architects or other designers.

- Take professional advice from appropriately qualified access professionals on the correct wording of design briefs and the preparation of access statements.

- Ask your architects or designers what degree of expertise they have. If they lack the appropriate expertise, seek alternative professional advice by appointing an access specialist to the design team. This access consultant should be independently and directly appointed by the client, not appointed by the architect.

- At concept stage, make sure you and the design team understand the fundamentals of inclusive access. These will not be limited to the design of the building, and will include for example:

    (a) the location of the building on the plot;

    (b) the gradient of the plot;

    (c) the relationship of adjoining buildings; and

    (d) the transport infrastructure.

- Liaise with the relevant statutory authorities as early as possible, and be prepared to amend concept designs as necessary.

- Keep suitable professionals involved throughout the design and construction process. Designs change during their gestation and need to be monitored.

- Be aware of the implications of different types of procurement route. Passing design responsibilities to contractors will reduce control of the result.

Think about how the completed building will be occupied and managed. Many barriers experienced at that stage can be overcome through good design.

Good Practice Point 19

p74

During the acquisition of a building, an occupier should seek appropriate advice and make a decision to acquire based on the existing levels of access, and if applicable the cost of improving access.

During the commissioning of a building, an occupier should set appropriate access standards through design briefs or employer's requirements.

During occupation of an existing building, an occupier should choose to improve existing levels of inclusive access by undertaking building alterations. Alternatively they can seek to relocate to a new and more inclusive building.

The use of examples taken from any development plan prior to its adoption is without prejudice to the Secretary of State's rights of objection or direction in respect of plan policies, or to call in plans for his own determination. The use of any example, whether from an adopted plan or otherwise, is also without prejudice to any decision the Secretary of State may wish to take in respect of any planning application coming before him as a consequence of a policy included in an example in this Guide.

Part 2:

Understanding
the issues

2. Introduction and background

2.1 The objective of this guide

2.1.1 The primary objective of this guide is to ensure the Town and Country Planning system in England successfully and consistently delivers inclusive environments as an integral part of the development process. An inclusive environment is one that can be used by everyone, regardless of age, gender or disability. It is discussed further in section 3 below.

2.1.2 This guide:

- provides guidance, information and examples of good practice, relevant to all participants in the development and planning process – local authorities, developers, occupiers, investors, access groups and disability organisations;

- introduces and explains the relevant legislation and policy frameworks, and in particular how the process of town planning must take a pre-eminent role in delivering inclusive environments;

- describes how local planning authorities can put in place appropriate planning policies and development control processes and suggests ways in which these can be best implemented and enforced;

- describes how developers, occupiers and investors can actively contribute to the delivery of inclusive environments;

- outlines the economic and social benefits of inclusive environments; and

- signposts other relevant literature and provides useful contacts.

2.1.3   The guide does not attempt to provide detailed and prescriptive lists of inclusive design requirements. That is the task of other reference material mentioned in the relevant sections of this guide. Whenever research is mentioned it refers to research undertaken by the authors in the preparation of the guide.

2.2   The nature of development

2.2.1   The development industry is diverse and thus the best way of delivering inclusive environments varies from development to development.

2.2.2   For example, major regeneration schemes in urban areas require a broad approach to inclusive design, addressing movement through public areas as well as the design of the buildings themselves. In contrast, a smaller scheme, such as the extension of a single building, has little or no impact on the wider public realm. The inclusive design approach here would focus on access to the building and movement within it.

2.2.3   However, whatever the scale and complexity of the scheme, the design and planning control objectives are universal – i.e. the successful delivery of inclusive environments. This is a realistic and achievable goal.

2.3   Who is this guide for?

2.3.1   Inclusive environments are the concern of everyone involved in the development and planning process, including:

- planning officers at development control and policy level;

- planning inspectors;

- councillors;

- developers;

- architects and designers;

- building control officers and approved inspectors;

- occupiers;

- investors;

- access officers;

- highways officers;

- English Heritage;

- the statutory fire authorities; and

- end users and members of the public, particularly disabled people, older people, women, children, parents, carers and anyone disadvantaged through poor design.

2.3.2   All of these groups will find this guide relevant.

Good Practice Point 1:

All parties involved in the planning and development process should recognise the benefits of, and endeavour to bring about inclusive design.

2.3.3   This guide does not apply in Scotland, Wales and Northern Ireland. However, the general principles will be relevant to those countries. It should also be noted that planning systems may change during the currency of this document. However whilst detail may vary, the principles established by this document will remain valid.

2.3.4   Neither is the guide relevant to modes of transport such as buses or trains, although it does relate to access and movement around public transport interchanges. It also relates to local transport plans. For further information on transport, refer to the guidance documentation listed in the appendices.

2.3.5   Changes to the current planning system are being proposed. This guide applies to the current planning system for development plan policies and development control. However, in placing great emphasis on effective engagement with local communities early on in the planning process the good practice advice contained in this guide is very much in tune with the spirit of the new proposals.

2.4 Terms used in this guide

2.4.1 This guide is aimed at all people involved in the planning and development process. Wherever possible, jargon and technical language have been avoided. However, there are a number of important and unavoidable terms with specific meaning relevant to the purpose of this guide. There is an explanation of these terms in the Glossary.

PART

2

3. An inclusive environment

3.1 What is an inclusive environment?

3.1.1 An inclusive environment is one that can be used by everyone, regardless of age, gender or disability. It is made up of many elements such as society's and individual's attitudes, the design of products and communications and the design of the built environment itself. It recognises and accommodates differences in the way people use the built environment and provides solutions that enable all of us to participate in mainstream activities equally, independently, with choice and with dignity.

3.1.2 An inclusive environment considers people's diversity and breaks down unnecessary barriers and exclusions in a manner that benefits us all. This is significant because although society and individuals have invested heavily in enabling people to manage their personal circumstances effectively (e.g. by caring for older people or providing aids and adaptations for disabled people), many people remain unnecessarily 'disabled' by ill-conceived environments. As a result many people cannot take full responsibility for themselves and are prevented from contributing to society.

3.1.3 This is best illustrated by looking at how the access needs of disabled people have been accommodated in recent years. Disabled people's needs are often considered separately from other groups of people and often after the design of a building has been completed. Solutions often lead to separate facilities, such as platform lifts or ramps for wheelchair users located on one side of a stepped entrance. Children's needs are often ignored altogether, for example, wash-hand basins in public toilets are usually too high. Baby changing facilities are sometimes located in the ladies toilet but not in the gents, preventing fathers from using the facility.

Inclusive access via the lower ground floor of this listed building was delivered through sympathetic and creative design, in discussion with English Heritage. The ground level immediately outside the entrance was subtly lowered to match the internal floor level and additional steps were added to the bottom of the curved external staircases.

This eliminated a short flight of entry steps and allowed inclusive step free entry and egress.

The Queen's House, National Maritime Museum, Greenwich

The original stepped entry to this building was remedied with an elegant solution that complimented the architecture of this listed building.

The existing steps were brought forward to a landing and ramped access was provided from both sides. This eliminated the need for a handrail on both sides of an asymmetrical single ramp.

The Treasury, London

A hard landscape design with a walk-through option for use by all. The texture's tactile surround defines the wet boundary of the feature.

Kerb free level access parking bays with a transfer area defined by surfaces, textures and planting. This avoids the use of painted lines on the road and pavement.

3.2 The positive impact of inclusive environments

3.2.1 Developing an inclusive environment will have a substantial and positive effect on society as an estimated 20% of the adult population, some 11.7 million people, have a disability. According to the Institute for Employment Studies (1999) their estimated spending power is £51.3bn.

3.2.2 There are two other important points to consider. Firstly this percentage is set to increase dramatically over the next few decades, as UK demographics shift towards an increasingly elderly population. Indeed, over the next 40 years, the number of people over 65 is set to rise by 40%, while the population as a whole is set to increase by only 7%.

3.2.3 Secondly and as described in 3.1 above, it is not only disabled people who benefit from inclusive design. There are currently a further 18 million people who would directly or indirectly benefit from inclusive access to buildings and public spaces. These include older people, families with children under the age of five, carers and the friends and relatives who accompany people with disabilities. Indeed it is fair to say that all members of society would benefit to some degree from intelligent, logical and accessible design.

3.2.4 In response to these powerful economic and social arguments, the government has long been committed to the creation of an inclusive society, where all people can participate fully as equal citizens. This requires social and economic, as well as physical, inclusion. In the context of this guide, the aim is to create a built environment which is inclusive to all members of a community. This relies on the positive contribution of all parties involved in the design, procurement and construction of buildings, those who occupy or invest in them, and those who grant or refuse statutory consents, particularly planning permission.

3.3 How aware of the benefits are we?

3.3.1 In preparing this guide, researchers have discovered that most statutory authorities have recognised, acknowledged and understood their professional and moral obligations for some time. This is an invaluable starting point, although progress to date in delivering inclusive environments is variable.

3.3.2 The research has also revealed that the commercial sector is increasingly aware of the benefits of delivering inclusive environments – it is aware of how significant the commercial benefits can be.

3.3.3 The commercial benefits can be summarised as follows:

- Developments designed to be inclusive are likely to have an enhanced market value as occupiers and other purchasers of property become increasingly aware of the economic disadvantage of excluding such a substantial percentage of the population. Occupiers now realise that inclusive environments are suitable for a wider range of people and are therefore more sustainable. Under the Disability Discrimination Act 1995 it is unlawful for employers (where they employ more than 15 persons) and persons who provide services to members of the public to discriminate against disabled people by treating them less favourably for a reason related to their disability – or by failing to comply with a duty to provide reasonable adjustments. This duty can require the removal or modification of physical features of buildings – provided it is reasonable. In deciding whether an adjustment is reasonable, both the costs and practicability of any adjustment and the financial resources of the employer or service provider would be considered. In relation to service providers this duty does not come into force until October 2004.

- It is significantly more cost-effective to provide for inclusive access at the design stage than to make retrospective adjustments during the construction phase or after occupation. Additional costs can be marginalised or eliminated if inclusive design is considered at an early stage.

- If a development is inclusively designed from the earliest concept stages, an application for planning consent is unlikely to be refused or delayed on the grounds that it does not meet appropriate access standards. This minimises the potential for delay, with obvious commercial benefits. In contrast, developments that are not inclusively designed will find local planning authorities enforcing the requirement for inclusive environments more effectively – the potential need for repeated applications and consequential delays will increase.

3.3.4   In summary, the delivery of inclusive environments will contribute to the government's wider social objectives, and will reward developers and investors by adding value to the building.

4. Progress to date in delivering inclusive environments

4.1 An overview

4.1.1 Success in delivering inclusive environments varies enormously between local planning authorities, developers, occupiers and investors.

4.1.2 Whilst there may be many examples of new public and commercial spaces and buildings that have reached the highest standards of inclusiveness, this has often been achieved by one of the parties in the process taking a leading role, with others having to follow.

4.1.3 However, there are still many inaccessible environments throughout the UK. In many cases this is because schemes have been granted planning consent without any party in the process properly assessing whether the scheme would result in an accessible environment. This highlights a need for everyone engaged in the planning process, including developers, to understand the importance of inclusive environments and of the opportunities which exist for creating them and to integrate the needs of all potential future users of the scheme.

4.1.4 This guide aims to address the situation by providing authoritative guidelines to steer all relevant parties through the planning, procurement and delivery process.

4.2 Common planning challenges

4.2.1 Our research has identified a number of recurring conditions or circumstances leading to planning permission being granted for buildings that do not achieve inclusive design.

4.2.2 These conditions or circumstances can include the following:

■ Many development plans contain few or no requirements relating to inclusive design. As a result, both planning officers and applicants tend to overlook the need to achieve inclusive environments. In some instances where development plans have not included a requirement for inclusive design, applicants have claimed that access is a not a material consideration, and have successfully appealed against a local authority's demands.

■ Planning officers and developers often see inclusive design as a Building Regulations issue, to be addressed once planning permission has been granted, not at the planning application stage.

■ The various statutory functions (planning, conservation/listed buildings, highways, and Building Regulations) are often considered independently or sequentially. As a result, potential conflicts in policy objectives are not properly addressed and opportunities for delivering common, effective solutions are missed.

■ Inadequate resource within local authorities often makes it difficult to invest adequate time to promote and enforce inclusive design. Consequently, levels of awareness are low.

■ Local authority planning officers often have little or no formal training in inclusive design.

■ Some local authorities may rely on local access groups who do not have regular and open lines of communication, or who themselves do not have appropriate professional skills and resources.

■ Even where inclusive design has been considered, it is often specific to the building, and does not include the setting of the building in the wider built environment. As a result, accessible buildings are sometimes located in inaccessible places.

■ Developers sometimes do not appreciate the economic benefits of maximising inclusive design, or they appoint a designer who is not familiar with the inclusive design approach. This lack of awareness on the part of developers and their advisers can result in a less accessible environment.

- The lack of appropriate national guidance to clarify these issues.

4.2.3   The following is a hypothetical example of how these circumstances might occur:

> A developer's proposal includes a ground floor slab that is raised 600mm above pavement level. The outline design is submitted to the local authority – perhaps without any pre-application discussion – and planning permission is granted. The relevant development plan lacks clear policy guidance on inclusive design, so the case officer does not raise this as an issue. Additionally, the local authority does not employ, or have access to the services of, an access officer.
>
> The scheme is then developed to the detailed design stage and Building Regulation Consent is sought. To comply with Part M and secure this consent, a compliant ramp has to be installed adjacent to the steps. This is duly added, but it undermines the overall inclusiveness of the access into the building.
>
> The result is a building that meets mandatory standards, but which is less accessible than if the ground floor slab had been lowered to pavement level in response to clear local authority guidance at initial planning stage – for both the developer and the local authority's officers.

4.3   Competing policy objectives

4.3.1   The core objective of delivering inclusive environments needs to be balanced against other policy considerations. Conflicts have arisen in the past between the following key pieces of legislation:

- The Town and Country Planning Act 1990.

- Planning (Listed Building and Conservation Areas) Act 1990.

- The Building Act 1984 and Building Regulations 2000.

- The Highways Act 1980.

4.3.2   For example, preserving the character of a listed building may appear to conflict with proposals to widen a door opening. Alternatively, a proposed ramp located on the public highway might be seen to constitute an obstruction. However, in most situations, a solution can be found which will comply with all the relevant legislation. Conservation officers and highways engineers need to think laterally and creatively. They need to work with access officers and access groups to find imaginative and innovative solutions that provide inclusive environments.

Part 3

Local Planning
Authorities – developing
an appropriate planning
policy framework for
development control

5. Developing an appropriate planning policy framework

5.1 An overview of the 'plan-led' town and country planning system in England

5.1.1 Reference has already been made to the importance of the town and country planning system in England, and to the development and planning process. It is important to fully understand this process, and how and why is it relevant to the successful, consistent delivery of inclusive environments.

5.1.2 The current planning system is based on primary legislation, orders and regulations. The legislative framework is provided by:

- Town and Country Planning Act 1990.

- Planning (Listed Buildings and Conservation Areas) Act 1990.

- Planning and Compensation Act 1991.

5.1.3 Every local planning authority is required to prepare a development plan for their area. This can be in the form of a structure plan (prepared at county level), local plan (prepared by district or borough councils) or unitary development plan (prepared by single tier unitary authorities, including the London Boroughs). The local authorities are also required to keep these plans up-to-date to ensure they are always relevant to planning applications.

5.1.4 Section 54A of the Town and Country Planning Act 1990 requires planning applications to be decided in accordance with relevant policies and proposals of the local authority's development plan – unless there are material reasons to depart from them. This is the 'plan-led' system of town and country planning that operates in England and Wales.

5.1.5 Because of this requirement, the single most effective way of ensuring the consistent delivery of inclusive environments during the development process is to include appropriate inclusive access policies in the development plan and to consider refusing planning permission to proposals that do not meet the necessary inclusive design standards. However, one alternative way forward might be through the use of conditions mentioned later in the guide.

Good Practice Point 2:

If a development proposal does not provide for inclusive access, and there are inclusive access policies in the development plan and any supplementary planning guidance, bearing in mind other policy considerations, consider refusing planning permission on the grounds that the scheme does not comply with the development plan.

5.2 Preparing appropriate development plans

5.2.1 When preparing a development plan, the local planning authority must take relevant national and regional planning guidance into account.

5.2.2 National and regional planning policy guidance is primarily set out in a series of Planning Policy Guidance notes (PPGs) and Regional Planning Guidance notes (RPGs). Appendix A provides a summary of current PPG advice relating to inclusive environments. Readers should however note that revision of PPGs is an ongoing process. The current list of guidance is therefore likely to change.

5.2.3 Our research has indicated that the most effective development plan policies will be those that include specific criteria relating to inclusive access throughout the whole plan – rather than just relying on a single policy. For example, a shopping policy could include a requirement for retail developments to be inclusively accessible as could an office policy, housing policy, and so on. These general policies should be supported by specific policies dealing with inclusive access. This approach helps integrate inclusive access throughout the plan, thus raising awareness and ensuring a consistent approach to all types of proposal. Stand-alone access policies are more likely to be missed and can also marginalise the needs of disabled people.

5.2.4   The insertion of appropriate policies in the development plan also ensures inclusive design issues are brought to prospective applicants' attention when they consider their development proposals against the development plan. In assessing whether a scheme is compliant with the development plan, applicants and their advisers will often test the scheme against every relevant policy. By having more relevant access policies, there will be more opportunities for helping to ensure the applicant considers whether or not the scheme will deliver an accessible environment.

5.2.5   Appendix C contains examples of development plan policies, which use a comprehensive range of inclusive access-related policies. It would be good practice for all local planning authorities to include similarly comprehensive policies in their development plans, tailored to meet their particular needs.

> **Good Practice Point 3:**
>
> Include appropriate inclusive access plan policies at all levels of the development plan supported by a specific strategic policy. Do not rely on a single access policy.

5.3   Supplementary planning guidance (SPG)

5.3.1   The previous section looked at the updating of development plans to include inclusive access requirements. In practice however it has taken some local planning authorities up to eight years to prepare their development plan. Even where development plans do exist, many of them do not refer adequately to inclusive design.

5.3.2   One solution to this is for local authorities to bring forward up-to-date guidance on specific policies through supplementary planning guidance. As long as this has been through public consultation, and conforms with and supplements existing plan policies and regional and national policy guidance it may be treated as a material consideration when assessing a planning application. In any event it is good practice for local authorities to prepare supplementary planning guidance dealing with inclusive access to clarify the detailed requirements of the plan policies.

5.3.3   Some examples of appropriate supplementary guidance are given below. Local planning authorities can also refer to the national design guidance and standards, identified in the reference section of this guide, particularly British Standard 8300.

5.3.4   Two examples are as follows:

One Local Council produced comprehensive SPG on Access and Facilities for People with Disabilities in November 1995. This comprised two parts: (A) Planning Policy and (B) Technical Design Guide.

Its mission statement is to:

- Maintain and improve the quality of life for people with disabilities and to

- Assist and educate designers, the construction industry and building, road and landscape providers to design, build and provide an environment which enables people with disabilities to participate in and contribute to life in the town.

In addition to including other policies within their plan, another local council adopted SPG on Lifetime Homes and Wheelchair Housing in April 2001.

This contains 16 design criteria to complement the UDP's housing policies. The criteria relate to issues such as minimising the distance between the car parking space and the main entrance, and providing living space at entry level.

5.3.5   The first example dealt with access in a comprehensive manner, whereas the second dealt with a specific aspect of access in relation to housing. These are examples of two different approaches.

Good Practice Point 4:

Develop and implement supplementary planning guidance as:

(a) the definitive inclusive design guidance of the authority or

(b) a way of ensuring that inclusive design is a material planning consideration without having to wait for the review or implementation of a full development plan.

5.4   Local transport plans

5.4.1   Local transport plans are a key component of the Government's transport strategy and are very relevant to the delivery of inclusive environments. Their purpose is to outline proposals for delivering integrated transport over a five-year period. Their potential contribution to the provision of inclusive environments is therefore significant. The preparation of these plans is the responsibility of the statutory highway authorities (SHAs) such as County Councils or Unitary Authorities. The various forms that SHAs can take are also discussed later in this guide.

5.4.2   Advice on the content of local transport plans is set out in **Guidance on Full Local Transport Plans** (DETR, March 2000). This guidance advises of the need to ensure that the decisions taken in developing and implementing a local transport plan take full account of, and complement, the land use strategy in the relevant development plan. Equally, the development plan strategy should underpin the land use issues arising from the implementation of a local transport plan. Inclusion of appropriate inclusive access policies within the local transport plan is therefore essential.

5.4.3   Ideally the development plan and transport plan should be prepared in parallel. However in practice this may not be desirable as transport plans are not subject to statutory procedures, and could thus be completed more quickly. Notwithstanding this, the overall aim should be to ensure that the overall planning and transport strategies are consistent in terms of inclusive design objectives and are compatible with one another.

5.4.4   Planning authorities and highway authorities should liaise to ensure that inclusive access policies are considered in sufficient detail in the local transport plan. Policies in development plans should be consistent with this guidance.

> **Good Practice Point 5:**
>
> Include relevant inclusive access policies within the local transport plan in co-ordination with similar policies within the development plan.

Part 4

Local Planning
Authorities – effective
development control in
the delivery of inclusive
environments

6. What is development control?

6.1.1   Development Control is the process by which proposals for development are assessed by local authorities against national planning policy objectives and the policies of that local authority (as set out in the development plan or developed in supplementary planning guidance). Following this process a decision is then made as to whether or not to grant planning permission in accordance with Section 54A of the Town and Country Planning Act 1990.

6.2   The process

6.2.1   After receiving the application, a development control officer will consider the proposal against national planning policy guidance, regional planning guidance, the local development plan and any relevant local supplementary planning guidance. He or she will liaise with colleagues in the planning policy team and consults with other statutory authorities such as the Highways Department. There are other stages in the development control process leading to assessment of the application, but this detail is not necessary for the purpose of this guide.

6.2.2   As part of this process the development control officer will recommend whether or not planning permission should be granted. In most significant cases a report will be prepared by the officer for the appropriate planning committee to consider. The report will indicate whether national and local guidance and policies have been met and consequently whether planning permission should be granted or refused. The committee will make a decision based on the planning officer's report and on further discussions and representations. This process should include an assessment of whether the scheme makes appropriate provision for inclusive design. The ideal way of undertaking this assessment and liaison is discussed later on.

6.3 Planning Conditions and Planning Obligations

6.3.1   For certain types of scheme, if the planning officer or committee recommends that planning permission should be granted, it may be appropriate for conditions to be attached to the permission to assist in the delivery of inclusive environments. These conditions might require improvements to be made in the local area in respect of inclusive access. An example is where access improvements are made to an adjacent local community building.

6.3.2   Alternatively, legal agreements may be employed to secure appropriate measures. Agreements under s106 of the Town and Country Planning Act 1990, which are generally known as 'planning obligations', can restrict a development or use of land in a specified way; require operations or use; or require the applicant to pay monies. With some schemes it may be necessary for legal or other reasons to secure inclusive environments through a legal agreement, rather than by condition. This might occur where an applicant is making a financial contribution to improve access to the site from other developments. Government policy on planning obligations is set out in DOE Circular 1/97.

6.3.3   It will be a matter for the local authority and applicant to determine which method should be used – condition or legal agreement.

6.3.4   However it is important to note that these agreements should not be seen or used as a way of enforcing inclusive access in the development itself.

PAR

4

> **Good Practice Point 6:**
>
> Consider the use of planning conditions or Section 106 agreements in enhancing the provision for inclusive access in the wider urban environment.

6.4 How closely are applications currently scrutinised for inclusive design provisions?

6.4.1 Our research highlights that inclusive design is often not closely considered by planning officers, for the following reasons:

- inclusive design is not seen by planners to be of relevance to planning applications;

- an absence of pre-application discussions means that applicants unknowingly submit inappropriately designed schemes;

- an absence of an up-to-date development plan or supplementary planning policy guidance on inclusive design means many officers do not raise inclusive design as a relevant issue; and

- a lack of planning staff with a suitable understanding of inclusive design means that many applications are not adequately scrutinised.

6.4.2 These factors highlight the need for strategic, 'joined-up thinking', with the local planning authority taking the lead role. To achieve inclusive environments through the development control process, three broad initiatives are suggested:

- working more closely with the applicant;

- staffing, training and liaison with adjoining authorities; and

- reconciliation of conflicting policy objectives, with the help of mediation if necessary – this is dealt with in Sections 9 and 10.

7. Working more closely with the applicant

7.1 Generally

7.1.1 There are three main opportunities to work more closely with the applicant: (a) pre-application discussions; (b) guidance notes, advising of the benefits of achieving inclusive environments; (c) a revised planning application form, encouraging the submission of access statements.

> **Good Practice Point 7:**
>
> Encourage pre-application discussions with applicants.

7.2 Pre-application consultations

7.2.1 Authorities should welcome pre-application consultations. The main benefits are:

- enlightening developers about the benefits of building inclusive environments;

- ensuring developers have the maximum possible time to develop 'accessible' schemes with the minimum disruption or amendment; and

- ensuring developers and local authorities have the maximum possible opportunity to liaise with third parties, such as access groups, and design the most appropriate solutions.

7.2.2 Local authorities need to make planning officers available for pre-application consultations, to make sure access is considered in the scheme. Unfortunately, resource is often a significant factor: many authorities do not have planning officers available to provide pre-application advice. Resource is discussed later in

PART

4

this section, along with mechanisms to place the onus on the applicant to ensure they properly consider access before they submit their application.

7.3 Guidance notes to applicants

7.3.1 Local planning authorities can emphasise to applicants the importance of inclusive access through guidance notes on the material needed to support applications.

7.3.2 The guidance notes should inform applicants of the need to consider access properly as part of their design and application. They should also provide a list of useful contacts and design standards. Authorities can also use the notes to encourage pre-application consultations with the appropriate officers.

7.3.3 The guidance notes will vary from authority to authority, and will reflect different policy considerations. However, they will generally refer to national policy guidance and appropriate development plan policies, and highlight when statements are necessary.

Good Practice Point 8:

Issue applicants with pre-application guidance notes.

7.4 Application forms

7.4.1 If necessary, local planning authorities should consider amending their planning application forms to include questions on how inclusive design has been considered as part of the development proposal.

7.4.2 By highlighting to planning applicants the importance of inclusive access, perhaps in the form of a checklist, local authorities can help raise the profile of access issues and ensure they receive the necessary consideration before submission of the application.

7.5   Access statements

7.5.1   Applicants should be encouraged to submit an access statement with their planning application. This would demonstrate the designer's commitment to take the issue of inclusive design seriously at the earliest stages.

7.5.2   The exact form of the access statement will depend on the size, nature and complexity of the scheme. However, each statement should identify:

- the philosophy and approach to inclusive design;

- the key issues of the particular scheme; and

- the sources of advice and guidance used.

7.5.3   In the case of existing buildings, particularly historic buildings, such a statement would enable a designer/developer to identify the constraints posed by the existing structure and its immediate environment and to explain how these have been overcome.

7.5.4   If an access statement is not submitted, local authorities might reject the registration of an application until such time as an adequate statement is submitted. This will overcome the problem of access delaying the 8-week deadline, as applicants will have to have addressed the issues before the application is made. This will also be a great incentive for applicants to consider access from the outset.

PART

4

8. Staffing, training and liaising with adjoining authorities

8.1 Generally

8.1.1 The raising of officers' awareness of accessibility issues through good quality training should go a long way in helping to bring about accessible environments. While this advice principally relates to development control officers, it also applies to development plan officers.

8.2 Staff training

8.2.1 As mentioned above, the single most effective way to ensure the consistent delivery of inclusive environments, is to consider refusing planning permission for schemes that do not meet the material considerations of the development plan or supplementary guidance. It is essential that development control planning officers and elected councillors receive guidance and training on this subject. If they are to assess applications effectively, they first need to understand what constitutes an inclusive environment.

8.2.2 If officers are to give the right advice initially – and indeed throughout the process – widespread and comprehensive knowledge of this subject is essential. Authorities should ensure that all planning officers have a proper understanding of, and be fully trained in inclusive design principles. They should be familiar with any supplementary planning guidance (which will conform with and supplement any existing plan policies) and the advice given in this guide. They should also keep abreast of any new government advice in this area. Other staff need similar training including highways staff, urban design officers and building control officers.

8.2.3 Properly-trained planning officers are the key to delivering inclusive environments. The responsibility for this rests with each planning authority.

8.2.4   The training of planning officers and other appropriate staff has a number of benefits. As well as sharing responsibility, authorities can integrate access issues as early as possible in the town planning process. They can also avoid access issues being marginalised or seen as an 'add-on' at a later stage – that is, as something only to consider after consultation on an application.

8.2.5   Raising awareness of access needs to start with the formal training of town planning, building surveying, conservation and highway engineering professionals. Therefore, graduate training courses (and other appropriate courses) should include basic access education in their core curriculum. This is a matter for individual professional organisations, such as the RTPI, RICS, and RIBA to review.

8.2.6   Including access as a subject for Continuous Professional Development (CPD) training will ensure planning officers and other relevant professionals maintain their awareness of the subject and of best practice, and are able to network with others. The Royal Town Planning Institute (RTPI) – and other professional bodies such as the Access Association – might consider taking a lead role in developing this initiative.

8.2.7   Our research also indicates the need for affordable training, as some courses and seminars are prohibitively expensive. For the RTPI, this may be through the branch office network. Well informed and adequately resourced local access groups need to work with local authorities to raise awareness in this area.

8.2.8   There is also clearly a need to raise awareness of access issues among planning officers, conservation officers, building control officers, engineers and local councillors – with initial and continuous training. This will improve consistency among local authorities, in terms of both the advice they provide and their access requirements of applicants and developers.

PART

4

Good Practice Point 11:

Make sure planning officers receive appropriate training on all aspects of an inclusive environment.

45

8.3 Access officers

8.3.1 Many local authorities already employ a dedicated access officer, and although it is not essential to do so, it is certainly beneficial.

8.3.2 In some cases, the access officer is consulted on almost every application for planning consent. While this may seem onerous, it is the most effective way of ensuring that a suitably qualified person checks every proposal's compliance with the policy objective. Other authorities only look at a small number of schemes, and these tend to be the larger ones. However, they all have an important role to play in co-ordinating the Council's training and consultation programme.

8.3.3 Some access officers are full-time, others part-time. Some were previously planners or building control officers, others have a community development (e.g. health promotion) or advocacy background. Some have personal experience of having a disability. The theoretical and practical expertise of access officers can vary enormously.

8.3.4 Each authority should consider appointing an access officer wherever possible. The resource implications, as well as the scope to share resources, and their required skills are discussed below. The suggested key functions of access officers are as follows:

- to assist in the development of appropriate access plan policies and design guidance, primarily through implementing supplementary planning guidance;

- to provide technical consultation and interpretation on applications that justify detailed input, and provide guidance to development control officers on when to consult;

- to be available for pre-application consultations on larger applications;

- to co-ordinate the consultation process with statutory consultees, such as English Heritage, Building Control and the Statutory Highway Authority;

- to co-ordinate and manage the Council's training programme for new and existing officers, in particular in development control;

- to liaise with neighbouring authorities and national bodies; and

- to establish a local access group where one does not exist, encourage and support the local access group and ensure that disabled people and other appropriate voluntary groups are effectively involved in the planning process. Servicing regular planning application consultation meetings and providing accessible transport and meeting rooms can be supportive.

Good Practice Point 12:

Seek to appoint an Access Officer. As a minimum, each authority should be able to call on appropriate professional advice whenever necessary – either through information and resource sharing with other local authorities or by the appointment of consultants with appropriate experience. Suitable consultants may be located through or be a member of the Access Association, or be listed on the National Register of Access Consultants.

8.3.5   The exact role of the access officer may vary from authority to authority – working in different departments in different positions. However the key objective is that, wherever possible, each authority should employ an access officer or at least have access to one.

8.4   Sharing resources with neighbouring authorities

8.4.1   Lack of local planning authority resources, including staff, often results in a lack of time for pre-application meetings. However, there are ways to overcome this.

8.4.2   First, neighbouring authorities can share resources and expertise by jointly employing an access officer/specialist. There are already examples of authorities working together informally, and this could be formalised to ensure all authorities can call on the services of an access officer, even if one is not employed directly by the authority.

8.4.3   Authorities could also make use of outsourcing by employing access specialists on major development proposals. While this may be appropriate in certain instances, it still relies on the authority having the budget, and is probably the least cost-effective solution. Authorities can obtain a list of suitably qualified organisations from the National Register of Access Consultants which is discussed below.

8.4.4   However, if the onus is placed on the applicant to show they have considered access issues (by submitting an access statement in support of the application), the workload and the resource requirement on the part of the authority will reduce. In most cases, a suitably qualified development control officer experienced in inclusive design principles may, in conjunction with members of the local access group, be able to decide whether or not the proposal creates an accessible and inclusive environment.

8.5   Sharing ideas, information and experiences

8.5.1   Local authorities could also take full advantage of the expertise available to them locally by establishing a forum for sharing ideas and experience. Access officers and other appropriate authority officers from a county or region could meet on a regular basis to discuss current issues and suggest solutions. Membership of appropriate organisations such as the Access Association (discussed below) and subscription to relevant publications would also help to maintain knowledge. Research shows that planning officers face common problems in dealing with inclusive design and therefore it helps to share experiences. This approach is already being adopted in one region.

> In one northern region a number of local authorities have jointly produced a Code of Practice on Access and Mobility. This gives detailed, technical guidance on access requirements across the county.
>
> As well as providing clear and consistent access requirements county-wide, the Code also helps to prevent developers going to a neighbouring borough or district with more relaxed access requirements.

8.5.2   For maximum benefit, other appropriate officers (such as planning and conservation) should be encouraged to attend the quarterly meetings. Alternatively, the forum could give a presentation to local authority officers and members on how to achieve a more accessible environment, and produce guidance notes.

8.5.3   As well as enabling authorities to share resources and experience, informal forums can ensure a particular region or area adopts a consistent approach to delivering inclusive environments.

8.5.4   The Access Association (formerly the Access Officers Association) may well have a role to play in any such arrangement. The Association, which was set up in 1991, is designed to network and support professionals responsible for promoting an inclusive environment and services for all. Members work in local authorities, as well as within voluntary and private sector organisations.

8.5.5   The Association could provide information on access officers and groups throughout a region.

Good Practice Point 13:

Share expertise and resources with other authorities as necessary. Set up regional or county access forums to network and share information across borough boundaries.

8.5.6   Planners can also keep up to date on access issues by reading about the case studies reported in journals such as Access by Design and the Access Association Journal.

8.6   The National Register of Access Consultants

8.6.1   The National Register of Access Consultants (NRAC) is a resource for building owners, occupiers, developers or planners seeking advice on an inclusive environment. It helps them to select reputable consultants who can demonstrate their credentials through their membership status.

8.6.2   Entry to the register is based on achieving certain skills, which are rigorously assessed through written submissions and at interview. These competencies concentrate on the knowledge of the design requirements and needs of disabled people.

8.6.3   According to the NRAC Client Guide there are two categories of full membership of the Register. They are Access Consultants and Access Auditors. Access Consultants are registered to undertake both problem-solving and problem-identifying work. The solutions to access issues that they are registered to provide may include technical advice where building structure or construction is involved. Access auditors are registered to undertake problem-identifying work and provide general advice on solutions.

The main distinction between auditors and consultants is that the consultant members have a higher level of construction knowledge. This is required when offering practical and feasible recommendations in relation to alterations to the physical features of a building. All Access Consultants are registered to undertake access auditing as well as access consultancy work.

8.6.4   The register is available online or in print. See the contacts section for more details.

8.7   Access groups

8.7.1   Most areas have an independent local access group, typically comprising local residents with physical or sensory disabilities. These groups can provide local authorities with a valuable service by giving them the benefit of their personal and practical experience. Many authorities consult their local access group on particular types of planning applications, but these relationships are often accidental, rather than formal. There are also opportunities for disabled people to join other groups to raise awareness in their community. The Royal Association for Disability and Rehabilitation (RADAR) have contact details for over 400 local access groups operating in England.

8.7.2   One City Council has a Disability Consultative Panel that meets every four weeks. The panel was formed in 1999 to comment on the access implications of a wide range of planning applications. With major development proposals, applicants are invited to make a presentation directly to the panel.

8.7.3   Access groups can, and do, provide local authorities with a valuable service, but these groups must be sufficiently diverse in their make-up. Officers (and members) need to consider the impact of a particular development on people with a wide range of needs, including people with physical and sensory impairments, older people, children and their carers and people with learning difficulties.

8.7.4   It is also important that authorities do not place too large a burden on access groups, particularly as they generally operate on a voluntary basis. Planning officers will need to consider the resources available from the group, and use these accordingly.

8.7.5   Ideally, each local authority should contact the access groups operating in their area, and work with the Planning Aid networks. This will allow them to understand the range of access needs represented, and establish how the local authority and the groups can work together to assess planning applications and raise awareness of accessibility. Regular meetings between disabled people and planners will help planners to understand the practical issues and become better advocates of inclusive design. If there is no local group, the local authority should set one up.

Good Practice Point 14:

Encourage regular liaison with local access groups.

8.8   Other decision-makers

8.8.1   At this stage, it is appropriate to note that some planning applications which have been refused may go to appeal and be decided by a Planning Inspector. Some applications are called in for determination by the Secretary of State.

8.8.2   Although the guide is not aimed specifically at Planning Inspectors, it is important that they should realise the importance of inclusive design and take the issue of accessibility into account in reaching their decision.

PART

4

Part 5

Combining the
interests of all
statutory authorities

9. Understanding the issue

9.1 Background

9.1.1 The effective reconciliation of potentially conflicting policy objectives, possibly by mediation, is fundamental to delivering inclusive environments and to ensuring that buildings and the spaces around them are accessible to all.

9.1.2 Negotiations and consultations with statutory organisations can help to identify conflicting policy objectives – both in the design of a scheme and the development control process itself. Conflicts usually occur at two key stages:

- Development control – at this stage, the objectives of statutory consultees, such as English Heritage and the relevant highways authority (not always the local authority), may conflict. While these organisations may have been consulted before the application is submitted, the formal process of consultation on an application is the crucial stage.

- Building regulation consent – the subsequent stage of applying for building regulation consent (which includes consultation with the relevant fire authorities) may reveal design inadequacies in a scheme that has already been granted planning consent. These flaws are often rectified to meet mandatory minimum standards, but not to achieve a fully inclusive solution.

9.1.3 Traditionally, both applicants and local authorities have dealt with these requirements in a sequential or unrelated manner. For example, English Heritage may be consulted at the planning application stage, and a compromise reached, but there may also be difficulties at the building regulations stage, thus making further compromise necessary.

9.1.4 The result of this is conflict, and the delivery of buildings and environments that fail to maximise their access potential. This is the result of a lack of 'joined-up thinking' mentioned earlier.

9.2 Getting results

9.2.1   The most effective way to overcome conflicting policies and to maximise accessibility is for all parties to consider inclusive design at every stage of the process, from inception to completion. This applies to two key areas: historic buildings/conservation, and highways.

9.2.2   Building regulation and fire precaution requirements should also be considered as early as possible. However, as mentioned earlier, it is not always possible to address these by liaising with a local authority's building control department. This is because of the increasing use of approved inspectors, discussed in Section 15.

9.2.3   Officers from different sections, departments or statutory functions need to be trained formally on how to deliver inclusive environments by design – and need to communicate effectively early on in the process. Authorities also need to work together more closely, particularly in areas with a two-tier system of local government. This is especially important with highways issues, as planning applications are usually determined by the district or borough council, while responsibility for highway matters is generally a county council function.

9.2.4   Local authorities should commit to a 'joined-up' approach along with conservation officers, engineers, building control officers (where relevant), planning officers and access officers in order to achieve access improvements. Officers and councillors should be encouraged to work together more closely to deliver a consistent approach. Two areas of potential conflict between the various statutory functions, and how to address them, are outlined below.

10. Statutory consultations with English Heritage

10.1 How and why might conflicts arise?

10.1.1 The Department of National Heritage (now the Department of Culture Media and Sport) and the Department of the Environment (now the Office of the Deputy Prime Minister) published the Planning Policy Guidance Note 15 in September 1994. One of its objectives was to provide pragmatic advice on applying conservation principles when undertaking work on historic buildings in a conservation area.

10.1.2 One of the strengths of the guidance is that it relates conservation to other objectives, and in particular to national policies promoting sustainable and viable economic growth. It acknowledges that there are only a few occasions where it is possible to preserve a building unchanged:

'Generally the best way of securing the upkeep of historic buildings and areas is to keep them in active use. For the great majority this must mean economically viable uses if they are to survive, and new and continuing uses will often necessitate some degree of adaptation. The range and acceptability of possible uses must therefore be a major consideration when the future of a listed building or buildings in conservation areas is in question.'

10.1.3 PPG15 goes on to say:

'It is important in principle that disabled people should have dignified easy access to and within historic buildings. If it is treated as part of an integrated review of access requirements for all visitors or users, and a flexible and pragmatic approach is taken, it should normally be possible to plan suitable access for disabled people without compromising a building's special interest. Alternative routes or re-organising the use of spaces may achieve the desired result without the need for damaging alterations.'

10.1.4 Although this guidance is positive, there is a perception that conservation and design officers in local planning authorities and English Heritage can be inflexible and generally do not support changes to historic buildings. While this view may be inaccurate, there are examples of conflict between conservation policies and proposals to achieve an accessible environment.

10.1.5 One example was a City Council's decision to refuse planning permission and listed building consent for a ramp to a listed building in the city centre conservation area. The details of this case are summarised in 'Access to the Historic Environment' (Lisa Foster, 1997):

'The entrance is approached via a short flight of semi-circular steps. The ramp would have risen from the level of the pavement along the side elevation and turned the corner, cutting into part of the steps which are a prominent feature. The diagonal line of the proposed ramp is emphasised by the handrails which would have cut across the existing decorative metal work. The appeal's inspector concluded that the diagonal line cut by the ramp and handrails would unbalance the architectural composition of this prominent city centre building.

The inspector characterised the proposed ramp and handrails as 'visual clutter' and judged they would unbalance the symmetry of the neo-classical façade. On this basis the inspector upheld the Council's refusal of listed building consent. The basis for the decision is that for a building where aspects of symmetry and balance contribute to its special architectural interest, new elements such as the proposed slope of the ramp – which do not harmonise with the existing design and which could potentially unbalance the classical façade – should not be permitted.

The inspector also found that the building's architectural interest contributed to the surrounding conservation area, so the proposed ramp to the front entrance would affect the setting as well as the building. This was cited as a second, and separate basis for denial of listed building consent.'

10.1.6 In this case, there was a clear conflict between competing policy objectives, and the conservation objectives were upheld. Indeed, discussions with various occupiers of listed buildings reveals a perception that it is generally the conservation objectives that prevail.

PART

5

10.1.7   The guidance in PPG15 contains a presumption in favour of the preservation of listed buildings. It also explains the legal requirement that special attention shall be paid in the exercise of planning functions to the desirability of preserving or enhancing the character or appearance of a conservation area.

10.1.8   Intrusive proposals need not necessarily fail the policy test of conservation or enhancement. Architects should think creatively in order to come up with acceptable solutions.

10.2   The role of English Heritage

10.2.1   English Heritage are given the opportunity to comment on a wide range of proposals affecting listed building and conservation areas in England and Wales. As a result their role is considerable.

10.2.2   English Heritage's officers are usually available to meet applicants for pre-application discussions, and there are specific guidance notes on this subject. Therefore, officers are well briefed and able to give detailed guidance.

10.2.3   Sometimes schemes to create inclusive environments have been opposed by English Heritage. Although individual English Heritage officers cannot direct that planning permission be refused, development control officers attach considerable weight to advice received from English Heritage. Where English Heritage recommend refusal, officers should explain why they reached this view and if possible suggest how any difficulties might have been avoided.

10.3   Pre-application discussions

10.3.1   With one policy objective that seeks to preserve or enhance listed buildings, and another that seeks to deliver an inclusive environment, proposals that require building alterations often result in conflict. The issue is how to meet both of these objectives.

10.3.2   The first method is to ensure appropriate policies are contained in the development plan and developed in any supplementary planning guidance.

10.3.3   Secondly, officers should work with the applicant earlier in the planning process to see whether it is possible to achieve creative, innovative and imaginative solutions that comply with both conservation and access policies. For example, an improved design or use of different materials could overcome the conservation policy objection.

10.3.4   Should any dispute arise relating to conservation and access policies when drawing up development plans or at application or appeal stage then mediation can be an effective way of resolving or avoiding these disputes.

10.3.5   Various funding sources, such as the Arts Council, require buildings to be designed inclusively if public funds are to be used in their development, refurbishment or regeneration.

10.4   Scheduled ancient monuments

10.4.1   It is worth mentioning that scheduled ancient monuments are different from most listed and historic buildings, in that their special interest is the key factor that attracts visitors. Unlike working buildings, alterations are generally not necessary to preserve the building or monument, and their economic value may be minimal.

10.4.2   Therefore for certain types of scheduled ancient monuments it may not be possible to achieve an accessible environment. However, every possible solution should be considered – including temporary facilities such as ramps – before reaching this conclusion.

PART
5

Good Practice Point 15:

Include appropriate heritage and inclusive access policies in the development plan, local transport plan and any supplementary planning guidance.

11. Statutory consultations with the Highways Authorities

11.1 How and why do conflicts arise?

11.1.1   Many improvements in inclusive access to buildings, particularly existing buildings, can be made by adapting the public highway. Therefore it is advisable that both planning and statutory highway authorities consider inclusive access in a co-ordinated way. For example:

- An applicant will often need to place a ramp on the public highway or raise the level of the pavement to improve access into the main entrance of a building.

- A new building may require additional transport infrastructure, ranging from simple amendments to a footpath, to a bus stop or new road.

- Inappropriate siting or design of the highway can cause obstruction to blind and partially sighted people. For example, parking cars on pavements obstructs pedestrians' free passage.

11.1.2   However, the responsibility for the adaptation, construction and repair of public highways throughout the UK does not lie with the local planning authorities determining the planning application. Instead, it is vested in a series of statutory highways authorities (SHAs) who may each have very different ideas on what is and is not acceptable. The local planning authority simply has an obligation to undertake a statutory consultation with the SHA.

11.1.3   The outcome can often be confusion or the unwarranted refusal of schemes that would enhance a disabled person's access via valid amendments to the public highway.

11.2 Background

11.2.1 To appreciate the reason for this, it is necessary to understand the differing forms an authority can take:

- **Motorways and major trunk roads throughout the UK**
  The Highways Agency – an executive agency of the Department for Transport, has responsibility for the principal roads throughout the UK.

- **Central and Greater London**
  Transport for London's (TFL) Street Management is responsible for operating and improving conditions on London's most important roads (the Transport for London Road Network). These roads (approximately 5% of the total) are mostly 'red routes' and carry approximately 33% of London's traffic.

  London's 33 local authorities manage and maintain those remaining roads outside the Highways Agency and Transport for London's control.

- **County Councils**
  County Councils are responsible for managing and repairing roads (with the exception of motorways and major trunk roads under Highways Agency control) throughout their designated region. A number of County Councils delegate this responsibility in part or whole to District or Borough Councils (see below).

- **District or Borough Councils**
  In certain circumstances, District or Borough Councils may be delegated responsibility to operate as a Statutory Highway Authority in their own geographical region.

- **Metropolitan or Unitary Authorities**
  Metropolitan or Unitary Authorities are responsible for repairing and developing roads (other than motorways or major trunk roads) throughout the geographical area of that authority.

11.2.2 This fragmentation of responsibility is a significant factor in the lack of consistent policy on public highways. It also means there is a lack of consistency in the way the SHA considers development proposals in their consultations with planning officers.

PART

5

11.2.3   The absence of a development control policy often leaves SHAs feeling ill informed and unable to deal with proposals appropriately.

11.3   Possible solutions

11.3.1   Planning officers should be aware that a large percentage of planning applications are influenced by the quality of access across adjacent land or the public highway. This is because of the obvious importance of reaching a building through the surrounding environment, as well as accessing the building itself once the front door is reached.

11.3.2   Therefore, the determining authority should develop policies and procedures in consultation with the SHA for assessing planning applications relating to public highways.

11.3.3   These should include appropriate liaison between the determining authorities and the SHA.

11.3.4   The policy should be developed at the highest possible level, for example at County Council level applying to all reporting district or borough councils.

11.3.5   The policy should address the following key issues:

- **The location and orientation of a building within a site:** if inclusive access is considered properly, it will often affect the positioning of a building within a site. Developers and SHAs need to be aware of this. In some circumstances, this may create more onerous requirements on the public highway.

- **Public liability:** many SHAs refuse applications that include a ramp with a retaining wall/railings on the grounds that resultant personal injury would be the liability of the local authority. However, in principle the installation of a ramp or the re-levelling of the pavement is no different to the installation of other street furniture. The measure of acceptability is effectively a risk assessment that will judge whether the works will prejudice free and safe flow of traffic or pedestrians. With new developments, appropriate location and orientation of a building in relation to the highway should negate the need to install a ramp, as level and inclusive access can be achieved.

- **Adoption or licence:** in some instances, SHAs may feel it is more appropriate to grant a licence or lease, and charge a peppercorn ground rent to a building owner who has placed works onto the public highway.

11.3.6   A number of councils have partially addressed this issue.
For example:

> One local council provides guidance on ramps on the public highway, which is also related to the Council's formal procedure and policy for dealing with proposals. It also explains when ramps will be acceptable and details design requirements.

11.3.7   It is recommended that more authorities consider doing this.

Good Practice Point 16:

Include appropriate highways policies in the development plan, and ensure these correspond with similar policies set by the statutory highway authority.

PART

5

12. Building regulation and fire precaution requirements

12.1 Building control: what it can and can't do

12.1.1 The purpose of building control is to secure the health, safety, welfare and convenience of people in or about buildings. As Part M of the Building Regulations deals with access and facilities for disabled people, building control rather than planning is often seen as the vehicle through which inclusive environments are delivered. However, Part M deals only with the minimum standards of design and cannot deliver a fully inclusive environment.

12.1.2 Before discussing further the potential limitations of building control in enforcing inclusive access, it is important to understand the background to building control and developers' obligations during the design and construction of a building.

12.2 Background

12.2.1 Building regulation consent is a mandatory element of the design and construction of a building. It derives from the Building Act 1984 and the Building Regulations 2002 (resulting from the Act) which apply to construction work undertaken in England and Wales.

12.2.2 The regulations are approved by Parliament, and Part M requires that there should be reasonable provisions for access to and use of buildings by disabled people.

12.3 Developers' obligations

12.3.1 If building work is subject to building regulations, under the conditions stipulated in the Act, a developer has a statutory obligation to secure building regulation consent. They can do this in one of two ways:

- submit an application to the local authority's building control department, who will review, and either approve (with conditions) or reject it, as appropriate; or

- use an approved inspector to review, approve or reject a design in the same manner.

12.3.2 Whichever route is chosen, the developer usually makes their building regulation application after planning consent is granted.

12.3.3 The principal reason for this late application is that the level of detail required for a building regulation consent is substantially higher than for planning – and naturally occurs at a later stage in the development process. Therefore a developer has nothing to gain by investing time and expense in accelerating designs to a detailed level until they have secured financial certainty in the scheme with a planning consent. They also have no statutory obligation to do so.

12.4 Working with the existing building control system

12.4.1 Planning departments and planning officers should aim to encourage applicants to consider their inclusive design strategy at the earliest possible stage rather than, as often happens, leaving such issues to be picked up by the building control process. There are a number of reasons for this.

12.4.2 First, the scope of building regulations is limited in both its content and the situations in which they apply. For example, the regulations may not apply in the following circumstances:

- some changes of use;

- temporary buildings;

- small extensions;

- certain small buildings; and

- special purpose buildings.

12.4.3   Secondly, even when the regulations do apply, the wider environment beyond the site boundary including pavements, bus stops, crossing points etc. are not covered.

12.4.4   Thirdly, the recommended solutions set out in the Approved Document which accompanies Part M of the Building Regulations aim to show applicants one way in which the requirement of reasonable provision can be met. They are not necessarily best practice and a more inclusive solution may often be achieved with fewer cost implications if considered at an earlier stage in the design process.

12.4.5   Fourthly, the increasing use of approved independent inspectors has reduced the opportunity for local authority planning and building control departments to discuss the access merits of a particular scheme. Where applicants have chosen to use an Approved Inspector they should be encouraged to ensure that liaison between the Approved Inspector and the planning department takes place at the earliest opportunity.

12.4.6   Fifthly, many potential improvements to a design may be undeliverable or hugely disruptive to the design process if not considered at an early stage. See 4.2.3. for an example of this. Practical improvements that can be introduced at this stage may result in a poorer quality of access than may otherwise have been achieved.

12.4.7   Finally, applicants will have to take account of the provisions of the Disability Discrimination Act 1995. The interaction between the DDA and the Building Act is explained in detail in the Disability Rights Commission Code of Practice 'Rights of Access: Good, Facilities, Services and Premises' paragraphs 6.6-6.8, (attached as Appendix E). Applicants are encouraged to see the advantage of adopting an inclusive design strategy as this should help to avoid the pitfalls that may exist in the grey area between building and civil rights legislation.

12.5 Recommendations

12.5.1 To achieve a fully inclusive environment, the inclusive design strategy must be seen as one continuous process starting with the initial design brief or master plan, through the planning process to the detailed design stage and building control approval. It is therefore good practice to encourage discussion at the earliest opportunity between planning departments and building control bodies.

Good Practice Point 17:

Encourage continuing dialogue between applicants, planning and building control bodies to ensure progressive development of the inclusive design strategy.

PART
5

Part 6

Good practice by developers, occupiers and owners

13. Developers

13.1 The benefits of inclusive access

13.1.1 Developers are becoming increasingly aware of the commercial benefits of delivering inclusive environments. As mentioned in the introduction there are obvious benefits:

- Developments designed to be inclusive are likely to have an enhanced market value as occupiers and other purchasers of property become increasingly aware of the economic disadvantage of excluding such a substantial percentage of the population. Occupiers now realise that inclusive environments are suitable for a wider range of people and is therefore more sustainable.

- It is significantly more cost-effective to provide for inclusive access at design stage than to make retrospective, post-construction adjustments. Additional costs can be marginal if access is considered at this early stage.

- If a development is designed to be accessible from the earliest concept stages, an application for planning consent is unlikely to be refused or delayed on the grounds that it does not meet appropriate access standards. This minimises or avoids the potential for delay – with obvious commercial benefits. In contrast, developments which are not designed to be accessible will find local authorities 'policing' the statutory requirement for inclusive environments ever more effectively – and the potential for delays will increase.

13.1.2 An accessible development is likely to have an enhanced market value. Owners or property buyers are now aware of their legal obligations both as employers or service providers to make reasonable adjustments to improve access for disabled people.

13.1.3   As well as the more obvious commercial benefits, there are less obvious ones such as 'market kudos' and 'brand awareness'. These have real value and many designers and developers have developed their businesses on them. Developers who fail to do so risk being left behind.

13.2   Effective process

13.2.1   How each developer ensures the consistent and successful delivery of inclusive access in each of their schemes depends on the unique characteristics of that organisation.

13.2.2   Below are a number of key principles a developer might follow to deliver an inclusive scheme:

Good Practice Point 18:

- Adopt a corporate policy that requires inclusive design to be part of all concept briefs to architects or other designers.

- Take professional advice from appropriately qualified access professionals on the correct wording of design briefs and the preparation of access statements.

- Ask your architects or designers what degree of expertise they have. If they lack the appropriate expertise, seek alternative professional advice by appointing an access specialist to the design team. This access consultant should be independently and directly appointed by the client and not by the architect.

- At concept stage, make sure you and the design team understand the fundamentals of inclusive access. These will not be limited to the design of the building, and will include for example:

  (a) the location of the building on the plot;

  (b) the gradient of the plot;

  (c) the relationship of adjoining buildings;

  (d) the transport infrastructure.

- Liaise with the relevant statutory authorities as early as possible, and be prepared to amend concept designs as necessary.

- Keep suitable professionals involved throughout the design and construction process. Designs change during their gestation and need to be monitored.

- Be aware of the implications of different types of procurement route. Passing design responsibilities to contractors will reduce control of the result.

- Think about how the completed building will be occupied and managed. Many barriers encountered at that stage can overcome through good design.

13.3 Appropriate design standards

13.3.1 Part M of the building regulations sets out the mandatory requirements that designers must comply with when designing a building for use by disabled people and others. However there are many other standards that will improve the quality of inclusive design way beyond the mandatory minimum. A number of these are listed in the reference section of this guide.

13.3.2 A key standard is the new British Standard BS8300, which covers many aspects of accessible design and should be an essential reference document for both designers and developers.

14. Occupiers

14.1 The benefits of inclusive environments

14.1.1 Occupiers have a commercial interest in residing in inclusive environments for the following reasons:

- Service providers do not benefit by excluding the large numbers of disabled people, older people, children and carers from their buildings. Major commercial benefits would be lost.

- Employers do not benefit by limiting their selection of employees to that part of the population that is not disabled.

14.2 Occupiers' liabilities – the Disability Discrimination Act 1995 (The DDA)

14.2.1 It is worth repeating that under the Disability Discrimination Act 1995 it is unlawful for employers (where they employ more than 15 persons) and persons who provide services to members of the public to discriminate against disabled people by treating them less favourably for a reason related to their disability – or by failing to comply with a duty to provide reasonable adjustments.

14.2.2 This duty can require the removal or modification of physical features of buildings – provided it is reasonable. Note that in relation to service providers this duty does not come into force until October 2004.

14.2.3 Market forces may as a result dictate that occupiers should favour buildings where levels of access take into account the requirements of the Act.

PART

6

14.3   Effective occupier policies

Good Practice Point 19:

During the acquisition of a building, a potential occupier might seek appropriate advice and make a decision to acquire based on the existing levels of access and if applicable the cost of improving access.

During the commissioning of a building, a developer or intending occupier might set appropriate access standards through design briefs or employer's requirements.

During occupation of an existing building, occupiers may choose to improve existing levels of inclusive access by undertaking building alterations. Alternatively they may seek to relocate to a new and more inclusively designed building.

Appendix A

Planning policy
framework

15. Town and Country Planning Act 1990

15.1.1   The statutory town and country planning system that operates in England is introduced in Part 3. However, reference is also made to other forms of national guidance. This is considered in this section.

16. National planning guidance

16.1.1   National planning advice is contained in a series of planning policy guidance notes. PPG1: 'General Policies and Principles' (February 1997) acknowledges the opportunity development proposals present for securing a more accessible environment for all. Paragraphs 33 and 34 state:

'Local planning authorities, both in development plans and in determining planning applications, should take into account access issues. These will include access to and into buildings, and the need for accessible housing. The internal layout of buildings is not normally material to the consideration of planning permission. Part M of Schedule 1 of the Building Regulations 1991 imposes requirements on how non-domestic buildings should be designed and constructed to secure specific objectives for people with disabilities. It would be inappropriate to use planning legislation to impose separate requirements in these areas.'

'... the developer and local planning authority should consider the needs of people with disabilities at an early stage in the design process. They should be flexible and imaginative in seeking solutions, taking account of the particular circumstances of each case. Resolving problems by negotiation will always be preferable, but where appropriate the planning authority may impose conditions requiring access provision for people with disabilities.'

16.1.2   PPG1 is therefore clear that developers and local authorities should work together to ensure that access issues are addressed at the earliest opportunity.

16.1.3   Additional guidance is contained, albeit briefly, in PPG notes on housing, town centres, transport and development plans. The first objective of PPG3: 'Housing' (March 2000) urges local planning authorities to 'plan to meet the housing requirements of the whole community, including those in need of affordable and special needs housing.' Paragraph 13 reiterates this.

16.1.4   PPG6: 'Town Centres & Retail Developments' (June 1996) identifies meeting the access and mobility needs of disabled people as a key issue (paragraphs 2.28). Paragraph 4.8 states that local authorities should seek to ensure that development is easily and safely accessible for pedestrians, cyclists and disabled people from the surrounding area.

16.1.5   PPG12, Chapter 3: 'Development Plans' (December 1999) deals with the content and level of detail of development plans. Paragraph 3.5 states clearly that 'development plans should not contain policies for matters other than the development and use of land (and should not contain policies which duplicate provisions in other legislative regimes, e.g. environmental health, building regulation and health and safety legislation)' although they should have regard to wider sustainable development objectives. Paragraphs 4.13-15 address 'social progress which recognises the needs of everyone' and acknowledges the need to consider the impact of planning policies on different groups of people, including those with disabilities.

16.1.6   PPG13 paragraph 19: 'Transport' (March 2001) refers to accessibility, but as with PPG6 it does not refer specifically to the needs of those with disabilities, although it does mention social exclusion in reference to those without cars. Paragraph 31 addresses mobility issues and paragraph 51 parking provision. Paragraph 82 refers to the use of planning conditions, for example, for securing parking provision for people with disabilities.

16.1.7   PPG15: 'Planning and The Historic Environment' states 'it is important that disabled people should have dignified easy access to and within historic buildings'. Fuller text is given in paragraphs 10.1.1 to 10.1.3 of this guide.

16.1.8   PPG17 – Planning for Open Space, Sport and Recreation – paragraph 18(ii) encourages 'better accessibility of existing open spaces and sports and recreational facilities, taking account of the mobility needs in the local population…'. Paragraph 20 states 'promote accessabilty……ensure that facilities are accessible for people with disabilities'.

16.1.9   PPG25 on 'Flooding' – paragraph 28 states 'raising floor levels (while ensuring that appropriate access is maintained for disabled people)…can enable buildings to resist and cope with flooding better'. Paragraph 35 comments that 'Sites vulnerable to rapid inundation should defences be overtopped or breached are unlikely to be suitable for those of restricted mobility, whether in conventional, adapted or sheltered housing or in institutional accommodation'. Paragraph 67 indicates that 'Consultation arrangements may need to make special provision for…proposed residential development, particularly for people of impaired mobility, in areas identified through development plan consultation as being susceptible to flooding, whether or not it is protected by flood defences'.

16.1.10   National planning advice therefore acknowledges the need to consider the impact of planning policies and decisions on people with disabilities without being too prescriptive about how this should be done.

Appendix B

Understanding
disability

17. Numbers of disabled persons

17.1.1   It is estimated that around 20% of the adult population (approximately 11.7 million people), are categorised as disabled under the definition of 'disability' in the Disability Discrimination Act 1995. In addition, another 18 million people will benefit from improved access into buildings, namely the elderly, families with young children and carers.

17.1.2   These figures are broken down in detail below and show the number of people who experience the functional impairments listed in paragraph 4 of Schedule 1 to the Act:

Type of disability	millions
Lifting and carrying	7
Mobility	6
Physical co-ordination	5.6
Learning and understanding	3.9
Seeing and hearing	2.5
Manual dexterity	2.3
Continence	1.6
Perceptions of risk	0.7
Numbers add to more than 11.7m as people could report more than one condition[1].	
Other beneficiaries will include[2]:	**millions**
People over 64 in the population	9
Families with children under the age of 5	3.3
Carers	5.9[3]

Source/notes:

[1] The Disability Discrimination Act: Analysis of Data from an Omnibus Survey; In-house report 30, Grahame Whitfield, DSS, 1997.

[2] Summer 1997 Labour Force Survey, UK.

[3] Caring about Carers, Department of Health, February 1999.

17.1.3   This group of people (more than 20% of the adult population) has substantial economic and social power.

18. The definition of disability

18.1 As defined by the Disability Discrimination Act 1995

18.1.1   The definition of disability in the DDA is fairly complex but, in essence, a person is regarded as disabled for the purposes of the Act if he or she has a physical or mental impairment which has a substantial and long-term adverse effect on their ability to carry out normal day-to-day activities. Full details of when a person has an impairment of this type are set out in Schedule 1 to the Act.

18.1.2   **Impairment** covers physical or mental impairments, including sensory such as those affecting sight or hearing.

18.1.3   The term **mental impairment** is intended to cover a wide range of impairments relating to mental functioning, including what are often known as learning disabilities.

18.1.4   A **substantial** adverse effect is something that is more than minor or trivial limitation, which extends beyond the normal differences in ability which might exist between people.

18.1.5   A **long term** effect is described as one which:

- has lasted at least 12 months;

- is likely to last longer than 12 months; or

- is likely to last for the rest of the person's life.

18.1.6   **Normal day to day activities** are activities which are carried out by most people on a fairly regular basis. This does not include activities that are normal for a particular person or group of people only (such as playing a musical instrument).

18.1.7   Examples of normal day to day activities are:

- mobility;

- manual dexterity; and

- physical co-ordination;

- continence;

- ability to lift, carry and move everyday objects;

- speech hearing or eyesight;

- memory or ability to concentrate, learn, or understand; and

- perception of risk or danger.

Appendix C

Examples of
suggested local
development
plan policies

19. Example policies for local development plans

19.1 Introduction

19.1.1 The following examples give an indication of the types of local development plan policies that might be included in local plans. They are not intended to be comprehensive and should be expanded or developed to suit the characteristics and structure of particular local plans. For example, additional policies might cover waterways, education, health and community facilities.

19.2 A strategic level policy

19.1.2 It is suggested that an over-arching, strategic development plan policy be included at high level within the plan. The wording might be as follows:

> **Inclusive access for all**
>
> The Council will require that, whenever possible, development proposals by virtue of their location and physical features meet the highest standards of accessibility and inclusion so that all potential users, regardless of disability, age or gender can use them safely and easily.

19.2.2 However, to further help create inclusive access, it is strongly recommended that references to inclusive access also be made at all levels of the plan. This can be achieved by adding relevant criteria to other policies, such as a shopping, transport or employment. As mentioned above, the following examples are not intended to be exhaustive, but are good examples of the type of policies that could be included in a UDP or local plan.

19.3   Built Environment

Inclusive access to public buildings

Development proposals (including extensions, alterations and changes of use) for any building that the public may use, will be required to provide safe, easy and inclusive access for all people regardless of disability, age or gender. This should include access to, into and within the building and its facilities, as well as appropriate car parking and access to public transport provision. Such buildings to include, but not be limited to, shops, restaurants, community buildings, health and leisure facilities etc. Supplementary Planning Guidance will be produced to give further details on how to integrate the principles of inclusive design into development proposals.

19.4   Transport

Parking for disabled people

In the case of non-residential development, the Council will require parking bays designated for use by Blue Badge Holders, located adjacent to or within easy reach of the main entrance and sized in accordance with BS 8300, 2001. The level of provision shall be in accordance with the Council's parking standards, with a minimum of at least one designated space in each development. Where no off street parking is proposed, applicants must demonstrate where disabled drivers can park in order to easily use the development.

In residential development the Council will require parking bays designed in accordance with the Lifetime Homes standards. The level of provision shall be in accordance with the Council's parking standards. Parking bays associated with Wheelchair Housing should be located adjacent to the front entrance, undercover, 3.6 metres wide and located beside a 900mm wide path connecting the front door, parking bay and the adjacent road.

Public transport infrastructure

The Council will require that any development that provides public transport facilities will provide safe, easy and inclusive access for all potential users, regardless of disability, age or gender. The opportunity should be taken whenever feasible to bring existing facilities up to the standards of BS8300, 2001 and to integrate the various transport modes in a fully inclusive way.

Pedestrianisation schemes

Any proposal to pedestrianise streets must incorporate parking facilities for Blue Badge Holders. The design and layout of street furniture should be in accordance with the Government's guidelines 'Inclusive Mobility' and the Council's Supplementary Planning Guidance on an Accessible and Inclusive Environment.

19.5   Employment

Access to workplaces

The Council will require that the highest standards of accessibility and inclusion be met in all developments that would result in the provision of jobs. Particular attention should be paid to public reception areas.

19.6   Recreation and leisure

Recreational pathways

The Council will identify a series of pedestrian and cycle routes linking areas of open space and leisure facilities and connecting to routes extending beyond the borough/district boundary. Where appropriate and where related to development, the Council will seek contributions for the establishment of new pathways and will encourage their use by providing information and clear signs at appropriate heights. These will improve safety and to provide better access for all potential users, regardless of disability, age or gender. Further details on the design of pedestrian and cycle routes and how to ensure safe segregation between cyclists and pedestrians can be found in the Council's Supplementary Planning Guidance on an Accessible and Inclusive Environment and in the Government's 'Inclusive Mobility' guidelines.

Sports facilities, arts and leisure buildings, hotel and tourist facilities

When considering proposals for sports facilities, arts and leisure buildings, hotel and tourist facilities, the Council will require that inclusive access is provided to all sections of the community, regardless of disability, age or gender. Further details can be found in the Council's Supplementary Planning Guidance on an Accessible and Inclusive Environment and in Sport England's design guidance, the Arts Councils access standards, and in standards produced by the Holiday Care Service and the English Tourism Council.

19.7   The public realm

The public realm

The Council will require that proposals to enhance the public realm and the pedestrian environment are designed to meet the highest standards of access and inclusion. Detailed standards on the layout of footways and crossing points including dropped kerbs, tactile paving and facilities at signalled controlled crossings, lighting, signage, public toilets and street furniture are included in the Council's Supplementary Planning Guidance on an Accessible and Inclusive Environment and in the Government's 'Inclusive Mobility' guidelines.

Access to open space and the countryside

The Council will require that proposals to provide or enhance open space and access to the countryside are designed to meet the highest standards of access and inclusion. Detailed standards are included in the Council's Supplementary Planning Guidance on an Accessible and Inclusive Environment and in the BT 'Countryside for All' guidelines.

Appendix D

Development Control
and Development
Policy flow diagrams

Developing an appropriate Planning Policy framework for development control

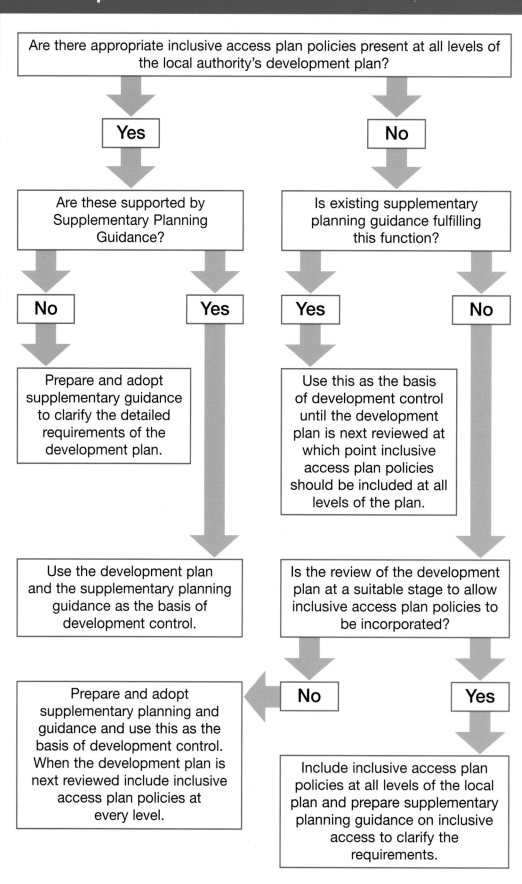

Are there appropriate inclusive access plan policies present at all levels of the local authority's development plan?

Yes

No

Are these supported by Supplementary Planning Guidance?

Is existing supplementary planning guidance fulfilling this function?

No

Yes

Yes

No

Prepare and adopt supplementary guidance to clarify the detailed requirements of the development plan.

Use this as the basis of development control until the development plan is next reviewed at which point inclusive access plan policies should be included at all levels of the plan.

Use the development plan and the supplementary planning guidance as the basis of development control.

Is the review of the development plan at a suitable stage to allow inclusive access plan policies to be incorporated?

No

Yes

Prepare and adopt supplementary planning and guidance and use this as the basis of development control. When the development plan is next reviewed include inclusive access plan policies at every level.

Include inclusive access plan policies at all levels of the local plan and prepare supplementary planning guidance on inclusive access to clarify the requirements.

Development control

Scheme conceived by developer.

Developer appoints appropriately qualified design or access consultant.

Outline scheme designed in accordance with the requirements of inclusive access.

Information packs and application forms requested from the local authority. Supplementary Planning Guidance and Plan Policy including Highways Policy, reviewed by designers.

Pre-application discussion between developer, designer and local authority officers (including access officers) who feed back comments and amendments as necessary. Where relevant pre-application discussions also held with statutory consultees.

Scheme revised if necessary and formal application to Local Authority in accordance with requirements listed on application form (including access statements).

Application reviewed by Access Officer, local access groups and statutory consultees.

Scheme considered by planning committee, inspector or secretary of state with inclusive access a material consideration.

Consent Granted.   Consent Refused.

Appendix E

Excerpt from the
Disability Rights
Commission Code
of Practice 'Rights
of Access: Goods,
Facilities, Services
and Premises'

20. The relationship between the Disability Discrimination Act and the Building Act

20.1.1   The following is an excerpt from the Disability Rights Commission Code of Practice 'Rights of Access: Goods, Facilities, Services and Premises'. This reference is referred to in section 12.4.7 of this guide. The reader is also referred to the full text of the guide itself.

20.1.2   **Paragraph 6.6:** Guidance is issued to accompany the building regulations. For Part M of the Building Regulations in England and Wales this is the Approved Document M. This sets out a number of 'objectives' to be met, 'design considerations' and technical details of design solutions (called 'provisions'). These provisions suggest one way in which the requirements of the regulations might be met but there is no obligation to adopt any of them. Most buildings will have followed the guidance in the Approved Document, but some will have adopted other acceptable design solutions.

20.1.3   **Paragraph 6.7:** Some disabled people might find it impossible or unreasonably difficult to use services provided at a building even though the building meets the requirements of Part M. In this situation, if a physical feature accords with the 1992 or 1999 Approved Documents to Part M, an exemption provided by The Disability Discrimination (Providers of Services) (Adjustment of Premises) Regulations 2001 (the '2001 Regulations') means that the service provider will not have to make adjustments to that feature if 10 years or less have passed since it was constructed or installed.

20.1.4   **Paragraph 6.8:** A building with features which do not accord with the effective edition of the Approved Document may have been accepted as meeting the requirements of Part M. If the feature is one which is covered by the Approved Document (for example, a lift) then, provided it enables any disabled person to access and use the building with the same degree of ease as would have been the case had the feature accorded with the Approved Document, it is unlikely to be reasonable for a service provider to have to make adjustments to that feature if 10 years or less have passed since its installation or construction. This is because the 2001 Regulations are not intended to deter people from adopting effective innovative or alternative design. Where a feature is one which is not covered by the Approved Document (for example, lighting) then under the DDA the service provider may still have to make adjustments to that feature.

Glossary

Access groups

Informal independent consumer groups, usually of disabled people, who work with local authorities and commercial service providers on a range of matters relating to inclusive access, including planning proposals.

Access statement

A statement prepared by an applicant indicating their approach to inclusive design.

Approved Documents

A series of documents suggesting one possible way in which the requirements of the Building Regulations 2002 might be met.

Approved Inspector

Private sector companies or individuals authorised under the Building Act 1984 to provide a building control service for all categories of work and for any building.

Building Regulations 2002

Regulations arising out of the Building Act 1984 applying to construction work in England and Wales. They are designed to ensure the health and safety of people in and around buildings, to provide for energy conservation and to provide appropriate Access and Facilities for Disabled People.

Building Regulation Consent

A consent formally indicating that a design proposal meets the minimum standards of the relevant sections of the Building Regulations 2002.

Determining authority

Usually the local planning authority who determine an application for planning permission, listed building consent or conservation area consent. In some cases, proposals may be determined by an Inspector following a public inquiry, and sometimes by the Secretary of State.

Development

For the purpose of this guide, 'development' means the carrying out of any building, alterations or operations that require planning permission (Section 55 of the Town and Country Planning Act 1990). This also includes changes of use.

Development plan

The development plan is rarely a single document. Once all the plans required by legislation are in place, the development plan for an area may comprise one or more types of plan depending on geographical location. Outside metropolitan areas these will be structure plans, local plans and minerals and waste local plans. Within metropolitan areas these will be unitary development plans (UDPs). However there are a few non-metropolitan areas that prepare UDPs and one example is the Isle of Wight, which is a unitary authority.

Disabled persons

The basic definition of disability in the DDA is 'a physical or mental impairment that has a substantial or long term adverse effect on an individual's ability to carry out normal day to day activities'.

Highway Authority

This is usually a County Council or a Unitary Authority. It is the authority responsible for the maintenance, cleansing, drainage and lighting of particular public highways.

Inclusive design

Inclusive design creates an environment where everyone can access and benefit from the full range of opportunities available to members of society. It aims to remove barriers which create undue effort, separation or special treatment and enables everyone to participate equally in mainstream activities independently with choice and dignity.

Local transport plan

Local transport plans are five year integrated transport strategies that cover all modes of urban and rural transport and link them together.

Listed building

English Heritage has the task of identifying and protecting historic buildings in England. The main means of doing this is by listing – recommending buildings for inclusion on statutory lists of buildings of 'special architectural or historic interest' compiled by the Secretary of State for Culture, Media and Sport.

Part M of the Building Regulations 2002

One of the 13 Parts of the Building Regulations that relates to Access and Facilities for Disabled People.

'Plan-led' system

The Government remains fully committed to the plan-led system, given statutory force by section 54A of the Town and Country Planning Act 1990. Where an adopted or approved development plan contains relevant policies, section 54A requires that an application for planning permission or an appeal shall be determined in accordance with the plan, unless material considerations indicate otherwise. This provides a framework for rational and consistent decision making. It also provides a system that enables the whole community – businesses, other organisations, and the general public – to be fully involved in the shaping of planning policies for their area, through public participation processes.

Planning policy guidance notes (PPG's)

In January 1988 Planning Policy Guidance Notes (PPGs) were introduced. The object of PPGs is to encapsulate concise and practical guidance in a clearer and more accessible form than Circulars. It is intended that PPGs will be the main source of policy guidance.

Scheduled ancient monument

To protect archaeological sites for future generations, the most valuable of them may be scheduled. Scheduling is the system that gives legal protection to nationally important archaeological sites in England by placing them on a list, or 'schedule'. **English Heritage** takes the lead in identifying sites in England which should be placed on the schedule by the Secretary of State for **Culture, Media and Sport**. A schedule has been kept since 1882 of monuments whose preservation is given priority over other land uses. The current legislation, the **Ancient Monuments and Archaeological Areas Act 1979**, supports a formal system of Scheduled Monument Consent for any work to a designated monument.

Section 35 (of the Highways Act 1980) Agreement

An agreement whereby a Statutory Highway Authority legally adopts a section of either newly constructed or privately owned (or both) highway, obligating that authority to maintain, cleanse, drain and light that highway, usually in perpetuity.

Section 106 agreement
An agreement under s106 of the Town and Country Planning Act 1990 that restricts the development or use of land in a specified way; requires operations or activities to be carried out in, on, under or over the land; requires the land to be used in a specified way; and, requires a sum to be paid to the authority on a specified date or dates periodically.

Supplementary planning guidance
Supplementary planning guidance can take the form of design guides or area development briefs, or supplement other specific policies in a plan. It must itself be consistent with national and regional planning guidance, as well as the policies set out in the adopted development plan. It should be clearly cross-referenced to the relevant plan policy or proposal that it supplements. It should be issued separately from the plan and made publicly available; consultation should be undertaken, and its status should be made clear. It should be reviewed on a regular basis alongside reviews of the development plan policies or proposals to which it relates.

Useful Contacts

The following is a list of organisations from which information may be obtained.

Access Committee for England (ACE)
Now the RADAR Access Advisory Committee (RAAC) – see below under RADAR

Action for Blind People
14-16 Verney Road, London, SE16 3DZ. Tel: 020 7635 4800.
Website: www.albp.org

Age Concern England
Astral House, 1268 London Road, London, SW16 4ER. Tel: 020 8765 7200.
Website: www.ageconcern.org.uk

Ancient Monuments Society (AMS)
Saint Ann's Vestry Hall, 2 Church Entry, London EC4V 5HB.
Tel: 020 7236 3934. Website: www.ancientmonumentssociety.org.uk

Architects and Surveying Institute (ASI)
Saint Mary House, 15 Saint Mary Street, Chippenham SN15 3WD.
Tel: 01249 444505. Website: www.asi.org.uk

Architectural Association (AA)
34-36 Bedford Square, London WC1B 3ES. Tel: 020 7887 4000.
Website: www.aaschool.ac.uk

BRE Advisory Service
Building Research Establishment, Bucknalls Lane, Garston, Watford WD25 9XX.
Tel: 01923 664664. Website: www.bre.co.uk

British Architectural Library (BAL)
Royal Institute of British Architects, 66 Portland Place, London W1B 1AD.
Tel: 020 7580 5533. Website: www.architecture.com

British Association of Landscape Industries (BALI)
Landscape House, National Agricultural Centre, Stoneleigh Park CV8 2LG.
Tel: 0247 669 0333. Website: www.bali.org.uk

British Board of Agrément (BBA)
PO Box 195, Bucknalls Lane, Garston, Watford WD2 7NG.
Tel: 01923 665300. Website: www.bbacerts.co.uk

British Council of Disabled People
Litchurch Plaza, Litchurch Lane, Derby DE24 8AA. Tel: 01332 295551.
Website: www.bcodp.org.uk

British Furniture Manufacturers' Federation Ltd (BFM Ltd)
30 Harcourt Street, London W1H 2AA. Tel: 020 7724 0851. Website:
www.bfn.org.uk

British Property Federation (BPF)
7th Floor, 1 Warwick Row, London SW1E 5ER. Tel: 020 7828 0111.
Website: www.bpf.org.uk

British Sign and Graphics Association
5 Orton Enterprise Centre, Bakewell Road, Orton, Southgate, Peterborough
PE2 6XU. Tel: 01733 230033. Website: www.bsga.co.uk

British Standards Institution (BSI)
389 Chiswick High Road, London W4 4AL. Tel: 020 8996 9000. Website:
www.bsi-global.com

Building Centre
The Building Centre, 26 Store Street, London WC1E 7BT. Tel: 020 7692
4000. Website: www.buildingcentre.co.uk

Building Cost Information Service Ltd (BCIS)
Royal Institution of Chartered Surveyors, 12 Great George Street,
Parliament Square, London SW1P 3AD. Tel: 020 7695 1500. Website:
www.bcis.co.uk

Building Maintenance Information (BMI)
Royal Institution of Chartered Surveyors, 12 Great George Street,
Parliament Square, London SW1P 3AD. Tel: 020 7695 1500. Website:
www.bcis.co.uk

Building Research Establishment (BRE)
Bucknalls Lane, Garston, Watford WD25 9XX. Tel: 01923 664000.
Website: www.bre.co.uk

Building Services Research and Information Association
Old Bracknell Lane West, Bracknell RG12 7AH. Tel: 01344 426511.
Website: www.bsria.co.uk

Centre for Accessible Environments
Nutmeg House, 60 Gainsford Street, London SE1 2NY
Tel/textphone: 020 7357 8182. Fax: 020 7357 8183. email: info@cae.org.uk

Commission for Architecture and the Built Environment (CABE)
The Tower Building, 11 York Road, London SE1 7NA. Tel: 020 7960 2400.
Website: www.cabe.org.uk

Chartered Institute of Building (CIOB)
Englemere, Kings Ride, Ascot, Berkshire, SL5 7TB. Tel: 01344 630700.
Website: www.club.org.uk

Chartered Institution of Building Services Engineers (CIBSE)
Delta House, 222 Balham High Road, London, SW12 9BS.
Tel: 0208 675 5211. Website: www.cibse.org

Chartered Society of Designers (CSD)
5 Bermondsey Exchange, 179-181 Bermondsey Street, London, SE1 3WW.
Tel: 020 7357 8088. Website: www.csd.org.uk

Construction Industry Research & Information Association (CIRIA)
6 Storey's Gate, Westminster, London, SW1P 3AU. Tel: 020 7222 8891.
Website: www.ciria.org.uk

Deafblind UK
100 Bridge Street, Peterborough, PE1 1DY. Tel: 01735 358100.
Website: www.deafblind.uk.org.uk

Disability Discrimination Act Helpline
See Disability Rights Commission

Disability Rights Commission
DRC Helpline, Freepost MID 02164, Stratford Upon Avon, CV37 9BR.
Tel: 08457 622633. Website: www.drc.gb.org

Disabled Living Foundation (DLF)
380-384 Harrow Road, London, W9 2HU. Tel: 020 7289 6111.
Helpline: 0845 130 9177. Textphone: 0870 603 9176. Website: www.dlf.org.uk

Department for Transport Mobility and Inclusion Unit

Department for Transport Mobility and Inclusion Unit, Great Minister House, 76 Marsham Street, London, SW1P 4DR. Tel: 020 7944 3000.
Website: www.mobility-unit.dft.gov.uk

Disabled Persons Transport Advisory Committee

Department for Transport, Local Government and the Regions, Zone 1/14, Great Minster House, 76 Marsham Street, London SW1P 4DR
Tel: 020 7944 8011. Website: www.dptac.gov.uk

Employers' Forum on Disability

Nutmeg House, 60 Gainsford Street, London, SE1 2NY. Tel: 020 7403 3020.
Website: www.employers.forum.co.uk

English Heritage

PO Box 569, Swindon, SN2 2YP. Tel: 0870 333 1181.
Website: www.english-heritage.org.uk

Federation of Master Builders

Gordon Fisher House, 14-15 Great James Street, London, WC1N 3DP.
Tel: 020 7242 7583. Website: www.fmb.org.uk

Help the Aged

207-221 Pentonville Road, London, N1 9UZ. Tel: 020 7278 11114.
Website: www.helptheaged.org.uk

Institute of Maintenance and Building Management

Keets House, 30 East Street, Farnham, GU9 7SW. Tel: 01252 710994.
Website: www.imbm.org.uk

Institution of British Engineers

Clifford Hill Court, Clifford Chambers, Stratford-on-Avon, CV37 8AA.
Tel: 020 7836 3357. Website: www.britishengineers.com

Institution of Civil Engineers (ICE)

1-7 Great George Street, London, SW1P 3AA. Tel: 020 7222 7722.
Website: www.ice.org.uk

Institution of Incorporated Engineers

Savoy Hill House, Savoy Hill, London, WC2R 0BS. Tel: 020 7836 3357.
Website: www.iic.org.uk

Institution of Structural Engineers (ISE)
11 Upper Belgrave Street, Lonodn, SW1X 8BH. Tel: 020 7235 4535.
Website: www.instructe.org.uk

Joseph Rowntree Foundation
The Homestead, 40 Water End, York, YO30 6WP. Tel: 0190 4629 241.
Website: www.jrf.org.uk

Landscape Institution
6-8 Barnard Mews, London, SW11 1QU. Tel: 020 7350 5200.
Website: www.l-i.org.uk

MENCAP
123 Golden Lane, London, EC1Y 0RT. Tel: 020 7454 0454.
Website: www.mencap.com

MIND, The Mental Health Charity
Granta House, 15-19 Broadway, London, E15 4BQ. Tel: 020 8519 2122.
Website: www.mind.org.uk

National Register of Access Consultants (NRAC)
Nutmeg House, 60 Gainsford Street, London, SE1 2NY. Tel: 020 7234 0434.
Website: www.nrac.org.uk

National Federation of the Blind
The Old Surgery, 215 Kirkgate, Wakefield, WF1 1JG. Tel: 0194 291313.

RADAR Access Advisory Committee (RAAC)
12 City Forum, 250 City Road, London, EC1V 8AF. Tel: 020 7250 3222.
Website: www.radar.org.uk

Royal Association for Disability and Rehabilitation (RADAR)
12 City Forum, 250 City Road, London, EC1V 8AF. Tel: 020 7250 3222.
Website: www.radar.org.uk

Royal Institute of British Architects (RIBA)
66 Portland Place, London, W1B 1AD. Tel: 020 7580 5530.
Website: www.architecture.com

Royal Institution of Chartered Surveyors (RICS)
12 Great George Street, Parliament Square, London, SW1P 3AD.
Tel: 020 7222 7000. Website: www.rics.org

Royal National Institute for Deaf People (RNID)
19-23 Featherstone Street, London, EC1Y 8SL. Voice phone: 020 7296 8000.
Text phone: 020 7296 8001. Website: www.rnid.org.uk

Royal National Institute for the Blind (RNIB)
Customer Services, PO Box 173, Peterborough, PE2 6WS.
Helpline: 0845 702 3153. Website: www.rnib.org.uk

Royal Town Planning Institute (RTPI)
41 Botolph Lane, London, EC3R 8DL. Tel: 020 7636 9107.
Website: www.rtpi.org.uk

Rural Design and Building Association
ATSS House, Station Road East, Stowmarket, IP14 1RQ. Tel: 01449 781307.
Website: www.rdba.org.uk

SCOPE
PO Box 833, Milton Keynes, MK12 5NY. Tel: 01908 645683.
Website: www.scope.org.uk

SENSE, The National Deafblind and Rubella Association
11-13 Clifton Terrace, Finsbury Park, London, N4 3SR.
Tel: Voice: 020 7272 7774. Text: 020 7272 9648. Website: www.sense.org.uk

Sign Design Society
66 Derwent Road, Kinsbourne Green, Harpenden, AL5 3NX.
Tel: 01582 713556. Website: www.signdesignsociety.co.uk

Society for the Protection of Ancient Buildings (SPAB)
37 Spital Square, London, E1 6DY. Tel: 020 7377 1644.
Website: www.spab.org.uk

Specialist Access Engineering and Maintenance Association
Construction House, 56-64 Leonard Street, London, EC2A 4JX.
Tel: 020 7608 5098. Website: www.saema.org

The Access Association
Walsall MBC, Civic Centre, Darwell Street, Walsall, WS1 1TP.
Tel: 01922 652010. Website: www.accessassociation.co.uk

The British Deaf Association
1-3 Worship Street, London, EC2A 2AB. Tel: Voice: 020 7588 3520.
Text: 020 7588 3529. Website: www.bda.org.uk

The British Dyslexia Association
98 London Road, Reading, RG1 5AU. Tel: 0118 966 2677.
Website: www.bda.dyslexia.org.uk

The Guide Dogs for the Blind Association
Burghfield Common, Reading, RG7 3YG. Tel: 0870 600 2323.
Wesite: www.gdba.org.uk

The UK Association of Braille Producers
c/o Royal National Institute for the Blind (RNIB), PO Box 173, Peterborough,
PE2 6WS. Helpline: 0845 702 3153. Website: www.rnib.org.uk

The Town & County Planning Association (TCPA)
17 Carlton House Terrace, London, SW1Y 5AS. Tel: 020 7930 8903.
Website: www.tcpa.org.uk

References

Access by Design – Journal of the Centre for Accessible Environments

Access for Disabled People: Practice Advice Note No. 3,
Royal Town Planning Institute (1988)

Access Journal – The Journal of the Access Association

Access Policies for Local Plans – Access Committee for England (out of print)

Accessible Thresholds in New Housing: guidance for house builders and
designers, DETR (The Stationery Office 1999)

Barrier-free Design – a manual for building designers and managers,
James Holmes-Siedle (Butterworth Architecture, Oxford 1996)

British Standards

- BS 4787-1: 1980 Specification for dimensional requirements of
  internal and external wood doorsets, door leaves and frames, British
  Standards Institute

- BS 5395-1: 2000 Code of Practice for stairs, ladders and walkways,
  British Standards Institute

- BS 5588-8: 1990 Code of Practice for means of escape for
  disabled people, British Standards Institute

- BS 5655-6: 1990 Code of Practice for selection and installation
  of lifts and service lifts, British Standards Institute

- BS 5776: 1996 Specification for powered stairlifts,
  British Standards Institute

- BS 6180: 1999 Code of Practice for barriers in and about buildings,
  British Standards Institute

- BS 6187: 2000 Code of Practice for demolition, British Standards Institute

- BS 6440: 1999 Code of Practice for powered lifting platforms for use by disabled persons, British Standards Institute

- BS 8300: 2001 Code of Practice for design of buildings and their approaches to meet the needs of disabled people, British Standards Institute

Building Act 1984 (HMSO, 1984)

Buildings for All to Use: Good practice guidance for improving existing public buildings for people with disabilities, Sylvester Bone (Construction Industry Research and Information Association (CIRIA) special publication 127, 1996)

Building Regulations 1991: Approved Document B: 'Fire Safety', 2000 edition, DETR (HMSO, 2000)

Building Regulations 1991: Approved Document M: 'Access and Facilities for Disabled People', 1999 edition, DETR (HMSO, 1999)

Department for Education and Employment

- Construction Standards (1997)

- Designing for Children with Special Education Needs: Ordinary Schools, DfES Building Bulletin 61 (HMSO, 1984)

- Designing for Children with Special Education Needs: Special Schools, DfES Building Bulletin 77 (HMSO, revised 1997)

- Access for Disabled People to School Buildings, DfES Building Bulletin 9 (HMSO 1999)

Department of the Environment

- DoE Circular 10/82: Disabled Persons Act 1981 (HMSO 1982)

- 'Housing for the Disabled' Design guidance handbook (HMSO, 1981)

- Development Control Policy Note 16: 'Access for the disabled' (HMSO, 1985)

- Regional Planning Guidance Note 3 (RPG3): 'Strategic Guidance for London' (HMSO, 1989 revised 1995)

- Planning Policy Guidance Note 1 (PPG1): 'General Policy and Principles' (HMSO, 1992, revised 1997)

- Planning Policy Guidance Note 3 (PPG3): 'Housing' (HMSO 1992, revised 2000)

Design Guides produced by local authorities:

Corporation of London	Designing an Accessible City: Offices, Julie Fleck (3rd edition, 1998) Designing an Accessible City: Retail Premises (1991)
Derby	Designing for Everyone, Department of Development Services, Derby City Council
Ealing	Accessible Ealing, Planning and Economic Development Department, London Borough of Ealing (1994)
Greenwich	Designing for Disabled People, Department of Planning, London Borough of Greenwich (1995)
Hounslow	Think Access – Designing for People with Disabilities, Planning Department, London Borough of Hounslow (1989).
Islington	Housing for People with Disabilities – a Design Guide, Technical Services Department, Islington Council (1989)
Leicester	Paving the Way – Design notes on accessibility, Stelios Voutsadakis Urban Design Group, Leicester City Council (1994)
Manchester	Designing for Everyone, Planning Department, Manchester City Council
Newham	No Barriers. Design Guidance Notes: Access for All, Department of Architecture and Planning, London Borough of Newham

Wandsworth   Access to Buildings and Spaces for People with Disabilities: Planning Policy and Design Guidelines, Technical Services Department, London Borough of Wandsworth (1989).

Westminster   Mobility Guide: A design guide for architects and developers, Planning and Development Department, London Borough of Westminster (1989).

Designing for Accessibility – an essential guide for public buildings, The Centre for Accessible Environments (CAE) (1999)

Development Plan Policies, Royal Town Planning Institute

Disability Discrimination Act 1995 (The Stationery Office, 1995)

Disability Discrimination Act 1995 Code of Practice: Elimination of Discrimination in the field of Employment against disabled persons or persons who have had a disability, Disability Rights Commission

Disability Discrimination Act 1995 Code of Practice: Rights of Access, Goods, Facilities, Services and Premises (The Stationery Office, 1995)

Disability Discrimination Act 1995, Part 4: Code of Practice for Providers of Post-16 Education and Related Services, Disability Rights Commission (2002)

Disability Discrimination Act 1995, Part 4: Code of Practice for Schools, Disability Rights Commission (2002)

Easy Access to Historic Properties: English Heritage (1995)

Fire Precautions Act 1971, Chapter 40 (HMSO, 1971)

Fire Precautions (Workplace) Regulations 1999 (HMSO, 1999)

Guidance on the Use of Tactile Paving Stones, DETR, (The Stationery Office, 1997)

Highway Act 1980 (HMSO, 1980)

Lifetime Homes Standard, Joseph Rowntree Foundation (2000)

Manual to the Building Regulations, The (3rd edition), DTLR (HMSO 2001)

Paving the way: how we achieve clean, safe and attractive streets, Commission for Architecture and the Built Environment and The Office of the Deputy Prime Minister: Research programme (2002)

Revised Guidelines for Reducing Mobility Handicaps: towards a Barrier-Free Environment, Institution of Highways and Transportation (1991)

Sign Design Guide: a guide to inclusive signage, Peter Barker and June Fraser (John Moores University and the Sign Design Society, 2000)

Tourism for All: Providing accessible visitor attractions, Bob Donaldson, (English Tourist Board, 1994)

Town & Country Planning Act 1990 (HMSO, 1990)

Urban Design Compendium, English Partnerships and the Housing Corporation (EP, 2000)

Widening the Eye of the Needle: Access to churches for people with disabilities, John Penton (Church House Publishing, 1999)

Wheelchair Housing Design Guide (Construction Research Communications Ltd – tel: 020 7505 6605).

Acknowledgements

The research and drafting of this guide was supervised by a Steering Group comprising:

Steve Marshall-Camm, Planning Directorate,
Office of The Deputy Prime Minister

Larry O'Neil, Planning Directorate, Office of The Deputy Prime Minister (project manager)

Mark Cousens, Urban Policy Unit, Office of The Deputy Prime Minister

David Petherick, Building Regulations Division, Office of The Deputy Prime Minister

David Rose, The Royal Town Planning Institute (RTPI)

Peter Lainson, The Royal Association for Disability and Rehabilitation (RADAR)

Keith Hamilton, Past President, Planning Officers Society

Andrew Shipley, The Disability Rights Commission

Darryl Smith, Access Officer, Bradford City Council

Peter Barker OBE, Disabled Persons Transport Advisory Committee

Tim Pope, Disabled Persons Transport Advisory Committee

Julie Fleck, Access Officer, Corporation of London